Divine Purpose

Myra Armstead

Myra Armstead

© Copyright 2019 Myra Armstead

No part of this book may be copied, scanned, printed or reproduced in any form or distributed without the written permission of the author.

Published by:

Editor: Mary Ann Herron

ISBN: 13: 978-0-578-52871-7

Myra Armstead

Special recognition to my mentors and author friends Stacey Yvonne Kimber (BFF) and Wendy Bass-Pickett. Thanks to the both of you for sowing so much into me. The both of you have inspired me encouraged me and supported me during my most difficult times.

TABLE OF CONTENTS

Chapter One
.... Humble Beginnings

Chapter Two
.... A Mother's Pain

Chapter Three
....Family Woes

Chapter Four
.... Desperate Measures

Chapter Five
.... Grief Strikes

Chapter Six
.... Accomplishments

Chapter Seven
.... Divine Purpose

Myra Armstead

Preface

Growing up Myra Armstead used to be a very bashful quiet girl with very few friends. She has never been one to open herself up to others. She has always been a person of observation. It was not until her adulthood that God started to clearly confirm how he wanted to use her to help others become saved and avoid life's pit falls. Myra has wrestled with spiritual instruction and confirmations.

She has experienced so much hardship, pain, and disappointments. The world has no idea of what God has brought her through and how He has brought her through.

Fulfilling God's purpose is my ultimate mission and goal; for the past three years I have been spiritually inspired to share my life encounters. God has been dealing with me regarding transparency. The things that I have experienced were not only for me. The trials, struggles and obstacles were also a testimony to help others. There are so many wounded people struggling in silence feeling that they are alone.

Myra Armstead

This book was inspired by various life changing events, situations, and circumstances. I am a firm believer in the saying "things do not just happen". My life experiences were necessary for a ***Divine Purpose***.

Prayerfully my encounters and experiences will inspire, motivate, encourage and most of all positively impact you.

Chapter 1

I often reflect back over my life sometimes by way of glancing through old photo albums. It has proven that as a little girl I was always loved by my parents and honestly somewhat favored. I was often referred to by my siblings as the "Golden Child". They assumed that I never did any wrong. However, they failed to realize that I used their mistakes as my guide of things not to do.

My mother gave birth to five children, her first born passed away within a year of birth. I was the third child next to the youngest. I was a product of my mother's second marriage. I have found so many notes and pictures validating that I was conceived out of pure love.

My father was a military man which caused for my parents to move around a lot. However, I was born in the City of Birmingham, AL and raised in Bessemer, AL. My parents separated during my childhood years and did not divorce until the year of 1994, which was my junior year of high school.

Myra Armstead

My mother found herself once again as a single mother and took on the role like a champ. I have never witnessed a woman work so hard to provide for her children. She never allowed her situation or hardships to defeat her. She made being a single mother with four kids look easy. I remember the hardships my mother endured like it was yesterday; which continues to play a vital role in my humility.

I recall my mother working countless hours, overtime, double shifts, weekends, holidays, etc. Sometimes she still did not have enough to cover all the household bills. My dad was active in my life and contributed towards my well-being however, our household continuously fell short.

I remember distant family members and friends giving us hand me down clothing in an effort to assist my mother. There were times I felt bad whenever my dad made his deliveries for me because my siblings were not as fortunate.

My dad never made me feel that he was not there. He always upheld his role as a father. He demonstrated love, spent time with me, provided for me and contributed towards my daily needs by being a provider. However, my mother still bore the burden of caring for three other children.

My mother provided us with the most important foundation of life... the love of God. We were required to attend Sunday School, church, choir unions and any other program on Sundays.

As a child I did not understand why so much church. I thought to myself this lady is crazy, even on my dad's weekend to have me she would make me return home by Sunday morning for church. Oh my gosh I use to be so mad at her. Whenever I visited my dad's house on the weekend it was so much fun and everything I thought I wanted or needed he had, which was the complete opposite from home. My dad had a daughter from a previous relationship. She was raped and killed at the age of 12. Her murderer discarded her lifeless body into an abandoned building like trash.

After I came along I can only imagine how my dad felt having a second chance at having a daughter. He definitely demonstrated it through his love and affection towards me. I guess that's why my mom found it necessary to name me after him. The bond my dad and I shared was immeasurable... the first man I ever loved.

As I grew older into my teenage years I can recall life's encounters changing and becoming more and more personal. I was starting to encounter my own struggles and no longer only witnessing my mom's struggles. On April 16, 1994, I was preparing for my high school junior prom. I had gotten all dressed up and awaiting my date to pick me up for our ritual multi house visits. My final stop for showing was my dad's house. He was so proud, so happy, so excited to see his only daughter dressed up in formal attire looking beautiful. He had a house full of guests including family, friends and neighbors. He was known to be one that loved music. He had the music blasting throughout the house people sitting around adoring our look for the night. I remember my dad giving his formal command for the night letting my date know what was expected of him and what would happen if he didn't comply.

Driving away from my dad's house in a red drop top mustang waving and laughing was the last time I saw my dad alive...

On April 24, 1994 seven days later my dad was murdered. His death was a result of a lovers' triangle that involved his newly married wife and her lover. This was devastating to me. I was only sixteen years old at this time and had to find out that my dad was deceased by a person who was present at the establishment where this horrific crime took place. My then stepmother's brother was the owner of this establishment. I cannot honestly say what happened to my dad that night. I have heard so many rumors and stories, yet have never received an explanation from any of the parties involved.

    I started to develop resentment towards my stepmother. Honestly at the age of 16 what is a young girl to do especially without any explanation as to why the love of her life is now deceased. I did not know how to express my feelings. I did not know who to trust because I felt that one of the people that I loved and trusted had betrayed me to the utmost. I recall as the days passed feeling the reality that my dad was gone… He was not coming back; my love, my protector, my provider. My mom was already struggling without help with my siblings and now I fell into the same situation. I remember falling into a state of depression. I was so sad and heartbroken. I cried every day multiple times a day. I was slowly falling into a dark place as I watched life around me with others continue. I remember losing hope, interest and a desire to move forward. Now as I reflect, I do not recall anyone being there for me, no one seemed to even care how my dad's death affected me.

My dad's family was very small. His mother, his dad and his sister predeceased him leaving behind him, his one brother and their grandmother. My uncle has four daughters and my deceased aunt had two children (two great-nieces). Outside of that my dad's family was complete. The Williams family was small but by GOD the love was so deep! This family is a family of love, hugs, kisses, encouragement, support and the list goes on and on. I found that being around my dad's family brought me comfort. However, I was still wrestling with the spirit of sadness, depression, anger, bitterness, as well as trust issues.

Being that my previously mentioned issues were not properly addressed I distanced myself from my brothers by my dad's wife. For some reason I blamed them for the situation because of their mother's association, which was not right. I was so upset and hurt by their mother's involvement in the entire situation. I was young yet understood that murder was a crime. However, the man that murdered my father never spent a day in jail which was even more gut wrenching. I just could not understand how it was ok to murder someone and not be held accountable.

Even though I was raised in the church, I did not understand how to seek God on my own behalf which caused me to be spiritually and emotionally lost for years. I truly understand now just how lost I was and the sad thing is I didn't even realize it at the time.

The tragic loss of my father created a sense of distrust for people, in which I'm still wrestling with to this day. I struggle now with allowing people in and have develop a stigma of not trusting people easily. I find that I have placed myself into a shell of protection where I know that only certain people are allowed. The pain of losing my father created a rippling affect in other areas of my life. I used to be so afraid to be happy after my dad passed.

For some reason I felt it was not fair to be happy without him. I did not realize at the time that to be absent from the body is to be present with the Lord. I continued to hold myself hostage. We can allow situations, people, circumstances and various things to hold us hostage. We must always trust God, trust His plan, trust the process and definitely know that there is a divine purpose for everything we go through.

Chapter 2

It's now time for me to graduate high school. Simply due to my own self-evaluation I knew that I was not a good candidate for a four-year college. Therefore, I decided not to go off to college. I strongly felt that I needed to stay close to my mom. She was my safety net and once again I did not trust many people outside of my household. I knew that I needed to do something so I decided to enroll into a local community college (Lawson State Community College).

I was so emotionally unstable I wasn't sure at the time what I wanted to pursue educationally. I think I later decided to enroll into the Business Administration program. I attended and continued this course of study for about a year. I eventually decided to stop attending school. I felt at that time it was best for me to work than attend school. So I started working at McDonald's and wasn't really comfortable but it provided some stream of income. Shortly thereafter I quit that job and started working at Wendy's and around this time I started back dating my now husband.

My husband and I have always known one another throughout childhood; he and my dad were neighbors. We had a hidden relationship before my dad passed. Due to the difference in age we both knew my dad would not approve of us dating.

A year after my dad passed away we started to date openly for a few years. During the course of our dating I became pregnant. I remember finding out and immediately becoming terrified being that I had trust issues. There were so many thoughts racing through my mind.

Even though I was a young adult I was still fearful of my mother and her reaction to this news. I always felt a sense of obligation to my mom. I never wanted to fail her or disappoint her being that I saw how hard she struggled to take care of us.

When I eventually told her that I was pregnant she wasn't excited. However, she wasn't mad either. Growing up in my household we did not express our love for one another we basically understood that we loved one another. I wouldn't encourage that because hugs and kisses are necessary. I still struggle to this day expressing my love. I am practicing more and more by telling and expressing my love towards others.

In the last trimester of my pregnancy I experienced complications which caused for multiple visits in and out of the complication center. I was miserable at the end. I eventually delivered my baby via scheduled C-section.

After delivery I was hospitalized for a week and a half and discharge with my baby girl. When I returned home, I remember feeling clueless, inexperienced, and scared as hell. I had a baby that was going to be attached to me from now on. My daughter's father lived only three blocks from me. Whenever he was not at work, he was there with us. Approximately two weeks after my daughter was born her father started looking for an apartment for us to move into.

I was praying the he didn't find anything because life's transitions were taking me on a whirlwind. It was like things were happening so fast. After about a week of searching he found an apartment and it was time to move. I felt it was noble of him to be adamant in stepping up to his responsibilities, yet I was scared to leave home. My mother didn't really want me to leave either and she was very quiet about the move. The baby and I moved out and life took off…

I was offered a job shortly thereafter with my local municipality (City of Bessemer) Mayor's office. God's favor superseded once again. Who can say that their first real job was with the Mayor's office? I was so excited and quickly acknowledged the blessings of God.

I recall the Mayor's staff taking me in like family nurturing, molding and grooming me in all areas of life and the professional work force. I was clueless about professionalism, business administration, professional writing skills, public speaking, the list goes on and on… reflecting back I thought that my immediate superior was so mean. I couldn't understand why she was so hard on me. I didn't realize at the time that God had a divine purpose for my life and she was part of the plan. During this time my faith and relationship with God was slowly increasing (Matthew 17:20).

Remind you I was no longer living in my mother's household. Being on my own forced me to increase my faith and retrieve all my tools that I had been provided with as a child (2Co 5:7).

As the years passed my life continued to mold and develop into the plan of God's divine purpose. Yet, I was still not spiritually mature enough to understand the process of God's plan for my life.

Divine Purpose

Throughout this time God started to send various people in my path to assist in developing me, guiding me in ways that I needed. I did not understand until now that it was all a part of God's divine purpose for my life.

Myra Armstead

Chapter 3

Life appeared to be going great. I had given birth to another daughter and maintaining stable employment with decent pay, my girls were getting bigger. My husband and I no longer worshipped at separate churches. We had come together as a family in its entirety. Things were great and appeared to be complete.

Just when you think or feel your life is going well, the devil is normally seeking the perfect opportunity to attack.

I will openly admit that I was the weakest vessel and I allowed the devil to take control. We continue to pray for God's protection and for the strength to endure throughout any and all temptations (Gal 5:23).

I found myself behaving in a manner that was not lady like most definitely not a characteristic of a married woman. I started to stray away from God and my family (husband & children).

Myra Armstead

I was so consumed with worldly and ungodly desires that I lost all focus and God allowed the devil to have his way with me and he did just that. We must be mindful of the situations we allow ourselves to get into. Hold to your spiritual principles at all cost because at the end of the day that is all that will stand in the end. I almost lost my family on the basis of my own selfish desires.

My family suffered from my decisions, keep in mind the decisions that we make affects everyone around us. Please do not be selfish like I was and think about your family and love ones. I created a situation of instability for my daughters, created a hostile and angry environment for my husband... My actions caused him to act out of character which I never publicly admitted. God is dealing with me on transparency.

There are countless people who are experiencing various situations that God has brought me through and my assignment is to share my story with intentions to inspire others. I am no longer ashamed of anything that I have encountered, endured, survived nor been delivered from because now I know that was a part of God's divine plan.

Divine Purpose

I have endured a lot throughout my marriage, but God has placed it in my heart for ME to be transparent and share MY imperfections. Never judge a book by its cover; you never know what a person is going through or has been through. Regardless of what is done to you, it is never ok to be disrespectful or dishonor your marriage. For the sake of it I could not understand why I changed, I was persuaded, why I willingly participated but now I understand that it was all a part of God's divine purpose. Yes, my disobedience was a part of the purpose. I am not perfect; no one is; God sent His only son to die in order to save mankind because He knew we were going to mess up. You see, God put all of us on a level playing field so that no one person would be more elevated than the other, which is why we are to love and uplift one another. After all, neither of us is better than the next. I know from personal experiences that I have been judged and sized up solely on my outward projection. There's only been a few who have taken the time to really get to know me or should I say genuinely interact with me. When we interact with others it should not be about us trying to figure out what you can get one to do for you; rather how can you help to better the next person. One of the ultimate functions of a Christian is to serve (servant). God has been ministering to my spirit for the past several years on transparency, which I have been wrestling with. I struggle so badly with trusting people. Prayerfully, you will understand why after reading this book.

I am required to share my story because there is no perfect person, no perfect marriage nor perfect family. I was 20 years old when I got married. I was clueless, not understanding the full concept of marriage. The Bible provides us all the instructions we need to sustain in life. We must turn to God during our trying times and not place so must trust in people. We put too much trust in people... remember once you open the door to allow others in they then feel entitled or obligated to know your business from that point forward. It is sad to say, but the ones closest to you will be the main people assisting in destroying you, your family, anything positive, and or thriving for you. Remember our FIRST person of trust is God and God alone.

I thank God for forgiveness, his agape love and restoration. God's purpose in this book is to demonstrate his power. You all see a Myra from the ashes but God want you to take a glance at the fire.

Chapter 4

Now my family has gotten back on the track. We are moving forward on a traveling train. After the last encounter, I honestly think the wind had been knocked out of all of us. Somehow it seems that we have a deeper appreciation for one another. When God rebuilds he rebuilds stronger!

Life is carrying on and even though we experienced damage from the train derailment, we are determined to work towards rebuilding in a positive way. The devil is mad now because he thought he had conquered my family and my sanity. God demonstrated his faithfulness and fought that battle for me and my family. The girls are growing up at a rapid pace I mean RAPID. One is about to be a high school graduate and the other one is entering high school. I am wondering to myself where did time go. I am reflecting on the lost time that I gambled and thinking of the failed ways I could have been a better mother. I have re-enrolled into school at a local university and obtained my

Myra Armstead

Bachelor of Science in Criminal Justice. Upon completion of my bachelor's, I enrolled into a Master's program of study and obtained my Master's in Criminal Justice. By this time I am working for the federal government, which led me to realize that I needed some sort of education that would assist in advancing my career opportunities. I then decided to enroll into another Master's program and obtained my second Master's in Public Administration, by this time I was second year law student at Miles Law School. During this time my mother was also diagnosis with dementia and became unable to care for herself. I was still determined not to give up even though so many obstacles were thrown my way.

Yet, God was demonstrating through me that your past does not dictate your future. My last year of law school during my second to last semester my oldest daughter was involved in a traumatic car accident. She was a passenger in the vehicle not wearing her seatbelt and was ejected. She suffered multiple injuries causing an extensive hospital stay with numerous surgeries and procedures. Once again, my family was being challenged. Desperate measures set in, I felt that I was experiencing an out of body experience. My daughter was so disfigured to the point that my husband and I both agreed not to allow anyone to see her in such state; no extended family members, friends, no one. For the simple fact that she had not seen the extent of her own injures; We felt as parents that we owed her the right to see and understand the seriousness of her own injuries before exposing her to others. We went through this journey for a month or so before she was released to go home. Thereafter, she was not able to care for herself. She was not able to walk for three months.

Even though this was one of the most horrible experiences ever. I still had to understand God's plan throughout the process. My daughter's injuries were consequences of her disobedience, because my husband (parent intuition) told her not to go with her friend, yet she found it necessary to go anyway. Just as we are as adults God gives us clear instructions and guidance, we still choose to do what we want then we expect God to bail us out. The decisions that we make bring consequences good or bad. It is important to pray for a sensitive spiritual ear so that you can hear God's guidance and warnings before destruction.

The accident seemed to have brought my family even closer because after the news settled and people were no longer curious the calls and visit attempts stopped and we quickly realized that we only had each other.

Chapter 5

Things started to settle after the life altering car accident. We have endured most of the therapy sessions and post medical visits. After three months off work both my husband and I started to alternate he would work one week and I would work the next ensuring that she had 24 hour care. My daughter eventually started walking again and slowly regaining her independence.

Being that my law school classes were at night I never stopped attending school except for the time she was in the hospital. Several months afterwards things appeared to be getting back to normal. Our household was starting to feel like we could breathe and have our independent lives back. We had been so consumed with home healthcare we had to rediscover ourselves. I felt that I was finally at a point where I felt that I could consume the moment of becoming a law school graduate. Honestly, I was so emotionally drained that I could not force myself to become excited. My support system seemed limited at the time. Nevertheless, I pressed forwarded working as hard as I could. Honestly, I had endured so much until my momentum was basically gone; not knowing that things were about to take yet another turn.

My oldest daughter now tells us she is pregnant. I was livid! My initial response was you can not have that baby. Your body is not healed, you are recovering from several broken bones, you are recovering from head injuries while recanting all the details and medical diagnosis the doctor had shared with my husband and me. Once again, my faith in God had diminished. I was stern in the fact that she could not have the baby. All my mind could think of at that time was it had not been a year ago that I almost lost my baby in a traumatic car accident and now she's delivering news that could possibly put herself at risk again. So here it goes again… our next two storms are brewing and forming worse than a category 5 tornado.

My daughter is furious at the fact we are not overjoyed, separation in the family occurs. Family rifts took place and the demonic force of Satan took reigns. People who do not understand spiritual warfare would not understand how the devil uses people and situations to destroy good. One thing for sure when you take things to God there is no betrayal or repeating of your wrong. However, when you find the need to seek validation and satisfy man that is when you will quickly learn that you are chasing your own tail in a circular motion.

I have grown to the point that it does not matter what others think of me or even say about me. My ultimate satisfaction is to God, the one and only who granted me salvation. When we as people stop searching for validation from others and stop seeking out to be accepted by society, then we will become more of the servant that God has called us to be.

Once again, when you experience various situations there is purpose in it, even if it is a not so pleasant situation, there is still a lesson God wants us to retrieve from it. God taught us through these hardships that no one is exempt, which is why we are to be compassionate and merciful when people are going through because you never know you could be next. We are not obligated to others' personal business however, as saved individuals we are required to pray, encourage and uplift one another.

I must admit during my daughter's period of rebelling she learned for herself the true character of people. She learned some valuable life long lessons about people, communication, character, privacy and the key element of silence.

I'm sure you are wondering by now, but she had the baby and I openly, publicly and proudly say that I have a beautiful granddaughter! I thank God everyday for removing the anger and disappointment and for allowing me to realize the blessing of being able to look into the eyes of little Ava. Please allow this to be a lesson for you. Do not allow fear and the unknown to take precedent over your FAITH in GOD.

During the time my granddaughter was preparing to enter this cruel world one of my closest family members was transitioning to be with the Lord. I was experiencing joy and sadness all in one within a 10-day time span. Angie was one of my biggest supporters, encouragers and most of all my confidant. She loss her battle to cancer March 5, 2018.

However, I am still emotionally grateful that the Lord allowed my mother to live and witness one of my most accomplished moments of graduating law school. Law school graduation was not the same. Angie was supposed to be present; sadly she passed exactly two months prior. My heart was crushed, I felt myself slipping into a dark place. She was the last closet relative on my father side of the family and it meant so much for her to see me fulfill my lifelong dream, which all derived from my father's death. I fought to remain strong for her daughter and myself for God is definitely a sustainer.

Myra Armstead

Chapter 6

One could easily categorize my up bringing as one of poverty. Yet before I was conceived in my mother's wound God knew his divine purpose for my life. I had been chosen before I knew who I was. Many had counted me out and wrote me off. Society formed an opinion based on how I looked, where I was from, where I worked, etc. God has the final say in who we are and what we become. I did not believe in myself for years.

I recall looking at my current life situations thinking to myself I might as well settle. Had I not experienced the things I experienced I would not be the person I am today. I thank God for everything he allowed to happen in my life even the most painful. One thing for sure everything that I have accomplished and achieved was nothing but God and His favor. God used me to break generational curses in my family.

I was I the first grandchild to graduate college with a Bachelor's degree. I was the first grandchild to finish graduate school obtaining two Master's degrees and I was the first grandchild to obtain a Doctorate degree.

I mention this because it is humbling that God chose me to be the one to make a difference. There may be some who do not like or may never acknowledge it, but God had a divine purpose for my life long before I was a thought.

Divine Purpose

Chapter 7

When it seems like the promise is dead. We must be willing to break free from comfort and trust God's plan for our life. Writing this book was VERY uncomfortable for me. Anyone that knows me know that I am a very private person; one who does not open up too quickly. God has been dealing with me in that area. There is a lot that he has placed in me that he wants me to share. People are looking at the outward appearance and judging along those bases, but very few seek out to get to know the inner person that lies within.

1Samuel 24: I thank God for creating me to be different for setting me apart. I thank God for the struggles and hardships I endured. God hid me in His plain sight for His own divine purpose.

I understand now that it had to happen; all my life's disappointments, heartaches, embarrassing moments, pain and sorrows. Remember God is a restorer. I lost everything when I say everything, I am speaking of peace, joy, hope, belief, confidence and the will... I lost it all.

I love ME all my flaws and imperfections. God has released a new being in me.

I do not regret anything I have gone through nor am I no longer ashamed of my failures. I understand that it was all a divine purpose to fulfill God's plan.

I have wrestled with transparency immensely for the past few years. God instructed me to be transparent, I now understand that God could not use me until I was obedient and open myself completely. Serving God requires surrendering yourself; I understand and acknowledge that my failures experiences and situations were for a purpose.

I pray and hope that I have served as a bridge via this book for others to crossover. I no longer seek validation from others. I know that I am enough within and through God alone.

This is my coming out. This is my truths, freedom and vindication from bondage. This is not the end; this is the introduction of a mountain of things God is about to do in my life for the benefit of others. I am God's vessel. I am chosen. I am HIS.

Dedication

Memory of my dad 'Myron (Ronnie) Williams"

I LOVE and miss you so much as I proofread the draft of this book, I became emotionally charged not from the pain; this time the tears meant something different. The tears meant vindication from the bondage of pain. Please know that you will forever live within me because I am YOU.

Memory of My guardian angel "Angela (Angie) Williams"

You were so many things to me, a mother figure, a sister, a cousin, a friend and even a corrector. I had so much planned for us, but God's plan was different. It is surreal to carry on with life without you. There is not a day that goes by and I do not think of you may even shed a tear or a laugh depending on the memory. I miss, love you so much... there is no word(s) that could describe the void and emptiness your physical absence has left. Anquanette, Laila and I will FOREVER keep your memories alive.

Myra Armstead

I dedicate this book to my best friend, my soulmate, my husband Marcus who is not perfect by any means but indeed perfect for me. You have stood the test of time with me. You have felt my pains, understood when others misunderstood, wiped my tears when the scars cut deeper than appeared and encouraged me when no one else was there; My two beautiful daughters Myia and Marlanda who have loved me unconditionally, as well as given me reason to have ambition and determination. I have not been the best mother at all times but you girls always made me feel as if I was the perfect mother. I LOVE you girls equally beyond measure; my bonus baby Ava Kay who has allowed me to experience love through an entire new set of emotions. You have afforded me and Papa a brand new level of Love; my God-Children: Micah and Eli who have been extremely patient and understanding of my neglect of time with them. I love your mom and the both of you beyond measure. You all have definitely enhanced my life. The fact that Stacey Yvonne thought enough to entrust you love bugs with me is truly a God send; my dearest mom Maggie who don't remember me but I vividly remember her love for us and all the hardships she endured to provide for her children (A

MOTHER'S LOVE). Ma I LOVE you so much. I can't put into words how your dementia has affected me. However, I am grateful to God for allowing you to be here. My loving and caring baby sister, Caprisia Williams who gives so much of herself - far more than she gets in return. I sincerely thank you for your unconditional love and limitless support in all that I do. Your willingness to alter your own life to care for our mother will never be forgotten. I am forever indebted to you. My guardian sister LaQuita Renea Evans for being everything that I lacked. You have been consistent throughout our entire friendship. You inspired me everyday I walked through Miles Law School doors even when I did not think I could do it. Thank you for every prayer, every call, every tear shed, every hospital visit… the list goes on and on. I pray God's richest blessings upon you and Aliyah. Golder Agee-Harris my sister you have cried with me so many days so many nights… you bored my burdens as they were yours, and I yours. The bond we share could never be severed. I Love You sweetheart.